Children and Narcissistic Personality Disorder:
A Guide for Parents

By Cynthia Bailey-Rug

Unless otherwise noted, all Scriptures are taken from the King James Version of the Bible.

ISBN: 978-1-329-71279-9

Dedication:

This book is dedicated to all who are attempting to help a child who has been harmed by narcissistic abuse, as well as those co-parenting with a narcissist. May God fully equip you with everything you need!

It is also dedicated to those who shared their stories and insight with me. Thank you for your valuable input on this topic!

Other books by this author:

Non-fiction:

Life After Narcissistic Abuse: There Is Healing And Hope

It's All About Me! The Facts About Maternal Narcissism

You Are Not Alone!

Emerging From The Chrysalis

A Witness Of Faith

Lessons From The Heart: What Animals Have Taught Me About Life And Love

All I Know About Marriage...I Learned The Hard Way!

Pawprints On Our Hearts

Baptism Of Joy

Romantic Inspirations

Facets Of Love

Fiction:

Sins Of The Father

The Christian Woman's Guide To Killing Her Husband

Table Of Contents

Introduction

Narcissistic Personality Disorder, or NPD, is so much more than a person being very selfish, as many people believe. It is a very complex, twisted and even sinister personality disorder.

Narcissists are completely self-absorbed. So much so, that they will not hesitate to use anyone in any way they see fit to accomplish their selfish goals. They will manipulate you, attempting to change how you see reality in order to keep you unbalanced (this is known as gaslighting or crazy making). This can make you doubt your sanity. They will destroy your self-esteem with the cruelest, harshest criticisms you can imagine. They will turn your family and friends against you, making them believe that you are the one with the problem, you are the abusive one or even that you are crazy. They will use you. They will take your money and/or possessions. In the mind of a narcissist, other people are on this planet simply to be used. People are more like a tool than a person in their minds, I believe. No one cares that they are using a screwdriver. That is the screwdriver's purpose, after all, to be used. They have no feelings on the matter. That is how narcissists treat other people, as if they are alive simply to be used however the narcissist sees fit, just like a screwdriver.

The insidious and evil nature of Narcissistic Personality Disorder means a person with it wreaks complete havoc in the lives of his or her victims. It takes many years to repair the damage done, and most often, it is never fully repaired. Often, the results of narcissistic abuse are only managed, not healed.

Did you know that the Bible mentions narcissism? It says it will become more common in the end times, which I believe is the time in which we are currently living. While it is not specifically called narcissism in the Scripture, this sounds like narcissism to me.

> *2 Timothy 3:1-5 " ¹This know also, that in the last days perilous times shall come. ²For men shall be lovers of their own selves, covetous, boasters, proud, blaspshemers, disobedient to parents, unthankful, unholy, ³Without natural affection, trucebreakers, false accusers, incontinent, fierce, despisers of those that are good, ⁴Traitors, heady, high minded, lovers of pleasures more than lovers of God; ⁵Having a form of godliness, but denying the power thereof: from such turn away." (KJV)*

It is obvious by the coldness and incredible lack of empathy so many people show these days that this is happening as we speak. This is why I firmly believe that everyone, and that includes children, needs to be aware of Narcissistic Personality Disorder, how to protect themselves from people with the disorder, learn about the devastating effects of narcissistic abuse and how to heal from them.

Children raised by at least one narcissistic parent can develop a myriad of physical and psychological problems as a result. Listed below are some examples:

- Low self-esteem.
- Feeling overly responsible for others, thus putting a huge amount of stress on the child which can result in physical and mental problems.
- Anger, either turned outward (as shown by abusing others) or inward (as shown by abusing one's self, such as with eating disorders or self harming behaviors.).
- Depression, often to the point of being suicidal.
- Anxiety. It can manifest in many forms such as Obsessive Compulsive Disorder, Social Anxiety, Generalized Anxiety Disorder or even Agoraphobia. Often it includes panic attacks as well.
- C-PTSD, also known as Complex Post Traumatic Stress Disorder, which includes a myriad of awful psychological symptoms including depression, anxiety, mood swings, irritability, flashbacks, intrusive thoughts, nightmares, hyper-vigilance, withdrawing from social situations, suicidal thoughts or actions. Physical symptoms can develop with C-PTSD as well. Pain with no known physical cause is common, usually in the lower back. Fibromyalgia, arthritis, digestive problems and heart problems also are

common. Sleep problems such as not being
able to fall asleep or stay asleep even with
medication are common, too.

- The child of at least one narcissistic parent
  may be abused repeatedly during her life.
  Growing up abused often makes a child think
  that abuse equals love, so she seeks out
  abusive romantic partners or friends. Also,
  growing up abused, abusers see her as easy
  prey. She gives off a victim "vibe" that
  abusers pick up on very easily.
- Inflammatory disorders are very common
  among adult children of narcissistic parents,
  such as arthritis and Crohn's disease. Other
  common physical problems are digestive
  issues, heart problems, kidney problems,
  diabetes and high blood pressure.
- Many grow up not believing in God or are
  angry at Him, blaming Him for the abuse they
  endured rather than the abuser. This can
  cause a child to grow up bitter and closed off
  to God.

Being raised by narcissistic parents, I am living proof of the
damage narcissistic abuse does, as I have lived with almost all of the
issues on the above list my entire life.

While being abused by another narcissist who is not a parent may
not cause as many of the above mentioned problems in a child as
being raised by a narcissistic parent, it still can cause a great deal of
damage. Narcissistic abuse is extremely damaging, no matter who is
doing the abusing. It is the most damaging when done by a parent,
however. I believe that is because parents have the most influence

over children. Basically, they are like God to a child, because they are where everything the child needs comes from, such as shelter, clothing and food. Also, children have a natural, in-born desire for their parents' approval and love, and they will do anything to gain those things. And, children also have another natural, in-born desire. That is to believe their parents love them, in spite of any evidence otherwise. Since children refuse to believe their parents do not love them, they will accept whatever their parents do out of the false believe that all parents always love their child, and do whatever is best for her.

Since you have purchased this book, it is safe to assume that you are not a narcissist. No narcissist would be interested in learning about narcissism, let alone teaching her children about it or helping them. Unfortunately though, I can assume that someone in your child's life has made you seek out this book. Whether that someone is your child's friend, relative, or even the other parent, I hope this book will help you to find ways to help your child. I hope it will help you as well. One thing I have noticed is it seems like you never can learn too much about narcissism. There is always something more to learn. And you do need to learn to protect yourself as much as possible from this evil personality disorder.

Also, while caring for your child, do not forget to take care of yourself as well, especially if the narcissist in question is someone that you must deal with regularly as well. The incredible stress of dealing with a narcissist can take a physical as well as emotional toll on you if you do not make it a point to take good care of yourself.

Simply for the purpose of making this book easy to write, to read, and since many parents I talk to are wives of narcissistic men, where it is appropriate, I will refer to the narcissist as "he" and the child as "she." If the narcissist you know is female or the child male, please do not worry - the information in this book is appropriate for either males or females.

If you have not read any of my books before, then you should know that I am a Christian, and will be offering some Biblical insight in this book. If you do not share my faith, then please consider continuing to read it anyway. I believe that the information in this book will help you whether or not you share my faith.

I am not a mental health professional. I am, however, someone with a great deal of experience with narcissists and their victims. This book includes the wisdom I have gained from my personal experience with narcissistic parents, an ex husband and in-laws, as well as input from people I have talked to who have had to co-parent with a narcissist or help their child who was abused by a narcissist.

Chapter One - Narcissistic Personality Disorder

Narcissistic Personality Disorder is a very complex and dysfunctional behavior, which can make it very difficult to explain even to other adults. The average person has difficulty understanding the incredible depths of the lack of empathy, delusions of grandeur and cruelty that narcissists possess because they are nothing like that. Even so, it needs to be explained to children for a few very good reasons.

First, since narcissism is on the rise, chances are very good your child will have to interact with at least one narcissist at some point in her life. She needs to be equipped with the knowledge of how to identify it quickly and how to deal with narcissists in a healthy manner.

If your child already has had the misfortune of experiencing narcissistic abuse, learning about Narcissistic Personality Disorder will benefit her greatly. It will show your child that what happened was not her fault, but instead the fault of the person who hurt her. She needs to know this so she does not take the blame for what happened, as that can cause a great deal of guilt, depression and shame. It also will help to validate her confusion and pain by giving a name to what happened.

Also, by having a name for what she has been through, if the child wishes, she can look up information on her own in the hopes of understanding her experiences better.

When discussing the narcissist, never talk badly about him, especially if this is your child's other parent or someone she cares deeply about. No child, no matter the age, wants to hear someone they care about being criticized. Criticizing him, even when it is well deserved, will make the child feel protective of the narcissist and possibly get angry with you. This only adds more complications to an already difficult situation.

Always remember, when discussing this very difficult topic, stay calm and collected. Your matter of fact demeanor will help your child to stay calm as well, rather than getting even more distressed. She will see that this is a real problem and not simply you being upset or moody. If your child sees you upset, she also could think that you are making this up or exaggerating. She can know you care that she was hurt, but she does not need to see you ranting and raging or calling the other person names.

Remember to state the facts as just that, facts. For example, if your child asks why Daddy feels so badly about himself, you can say something like it is because he did not feel loved enough when he was a little boy. It left a hole in his heart that he tries to fill up in other ways. That response simply explains the problem without criticizing the child's father or his parents, for that matter. It simply says that is how he felt, and this is what he has done about it.

The following section includes some suggestions on how to explain narcissism in very simplified terms that even young children can understand. I know there is a lot of information here, and it can be quite overwhelming just thinking about discussing this with your child. Take a few deep breaths and relax. You can do this! Please feel free to change this information however you feel it is most appropriate for your child. Or, leave some of it out to discuss at a future time, if you feel that is the right thing to do. It can be a lot to absorb, so you may need to talk about it in small doses. You know your child best, after all, so you will know the best way to talk about this topic. I also would like to urge you to pray before talking to your child, though, and follow God's promptings on this matter. And, ask Him to give you the right words. He truly will guide you in the right direction on this difficult topic!

Narcissists do not like themselves. They treat other people badly because it makes them feel better about themselves. They think this is the only way they can feel good about themselves, because they never learned healthy ways to do it, like talking to God about how they feel.

They are always afraid that people will find out that they are bad. Everything they do is about how they feel about themselves. They try to make sure no one knows they are the bad people they think they are, and at the same time, they try to make themselves feel better about themselves. This is why they behave so poorly. They think so much about how they feel about themselves and what people think of them, they do not think about the fact they are hurting people. Then there are other times that they do know they are hurting people, but they want so badly to feel good, that it matters more to them than them hurting someone else.

Narcissists think other people need to make them feel better about themselves since they cannot do it.

Because they feel so badly about themselves, they do not admit when they have done something wrong or hurtful. It would make them feel even worse to admit that they did something bad. That is why they blame other people when they are the ones who have done something bad.

They also need a lot of attention, because it makes them feel good about themselves when a lot of people are paying attention to them.

There are two types of narcissists. They are called overt and covert narcissists. Overt narcissists are the "in your face" type. They act very boldly, and tend to be show offs. Covert narcissists are much quieter. They act helpless, like they cannot understand or do certain things. They want people to do things for them and to take care of them. If they do something mean to you, often they will pretend they did not know it would hurt you, then act like you are mean for saying something to them about what they did.

Narcissists brag about any good things they have done, because they think it makes other people think they are really great. They seem to think if they brag enough, other people will believe they are as smart or talented as they say they are.

They do not like people who they think look better than them, or who are smarter or richer, because they feel the other person makes them look bad.

Narcissistic supply is what it is called when someone makes a narcissist feel better about himself. If a person stops giving that supply, the narcissist may stop talking to that person. While it is good to complement people, that does not mean it is your job to make another person feel better about himself, even though he may act like it is. How he feels about himself is between him and God.

Narcissists think how a person looks is more important than the kind of person she is. They think how a person looks means the person is good or bad. They do not realize that a bad person can dress nicely or a good person can wear worn out clothes.

It makes narcissists feel powerful to make a person do something, especially when it is something she does not want to do. They can make you think some things are right or true, when they are not, or they will make you think bad things are good when they are not (this is called gaslighting or crazy making). They will say and do all kinds of things to make a person do what they want. They may stop speaking to you or threaten you. Threats do not always have to be spoken. They can involve a mean look or a certain tone of voice.

Sometimes narcissists say things to make you feel like you have to take care of them like, "I need you!" "I can't talk to anyone else about this!" (Note for parents: guilt is to encourage the victim to take care of the narcissist. When this is done by an adult to a child, this type of co-dependent behavior turns into what is known as emotional incest, covert incest or parentalizing. All three terms mean the exact same thing – when a parent expects the child to take care of him rather than the parent taking care of the child. Such abuse can cause devastating effects on a child's mental health. It will be discussed in more detail in the following chapter.)

When a narcissist is upset with you, he may get someone else to try to make you see things his way. That other person may tell you that you are wrong or you need to make the problem right. This is called triangulation, and it is not right. Mature, safe people talk directly to the person they are upset with to work things out together. They do not involve other people.

Children are naturally curious, so chances are your child will want to ask you some questions no matter how thoroughly you explained Narcissistic Personality Disorder. When answering the questions, lean on God for help. He truly will guide you in the right way to say things.

Chapter Two – Repairing The Damage

Children need to know more than just details about Narcissistic Personality Disorder. They need to know the have the right to protect themselves from narcissists and that the abuse is not their fault. They also need help to heal. In this chapter, I will cover those topics.

Children need to know what love truly is in order to fully understand her right to protect herself as well as how to treat others. Love for herself as well as love for others will help her to have healthy relationships.

1 Corinthians 13:1-7 explains love beautifully. I am including it below. Feel free to use these verses as an example on discussing what love truly is to your child.

> *"Though I speak with the tongues of men and of angels, and have not charity, I am become as sounding brass, or a tinkling cymbal.* ² *And though I have the gift of prophecy, and understand all mysteries, and all knowledge; and though I have all faith, so that I could remove mountains, and have not charity, I am nothing.* ³ *And though I bestow all my goods to feed the poor, and*

though I give my body to be burned, and have not charity, it profiteth me nothing.

⁴Charity suffereth long, and is kind; charity envieth not; charity vaunteth not itself, is not puffed up, ⁵ Doth not behave itself unseemly, seeketh not her own, is not easily provoked, thinketh no evil; ⁶ Rejoiceth not in iniquity, but rejoiceth in the truth; ⁷ Beareth all things, believeth all things, hopeth all things, endureth all things."
(KJV)

Make sure you child knows that although she may love the narcissist, that does not mean she has to tolerate being abused. Love wants what is best for people, and letting someone mistreat you is not love for you or the other person. **Tolerating abuse is never love.** It means that you are letting someone treat you badly instead of encouraging them to behave well. While you cannot force a person to behave properly, at least you can set the stage for them to do so by telling them you do not like how they are treating you and setting and enforcing good boundaries. Plus, tolerating abuse means you are essentially telling yourself that you are not worthy of being treated well. Over time, that hurts or even devastates your self-esteem.

Make sure your child knows that whatever the narcissistic person does to her is not her fault. Nothing she has said or done has made the narcissist act that way. Something is wrong with him, not with the people he hurts. How a person acts is that person's responsibility, no one else's! You may need to repeat this often, as self-blame can run deeply in children. I grew up convinced my mother abusing me was my fault, and carried this belief well into my adulthood. Frankly, it is a terrible, miserable way to feel. I would not wish that on anybody!

Acknowledge that what happened to your child was abuse. Validate her pain and confusion. So many victims of narcissistic abuse of all ages invalidate their own pain, saying it was not so bad because the narcissist did not hit them or other people have it worse. This only creates more suffering and damages the self-esteem.

Your child is also not bad for how she may feel. It is perfectly normal to feel bad when someone is mean to them. It is also perfectly normal to feel confused. Narcissists are very confusing people! Urge your child to talk about her feelings, and reassure her that she is normal for what she feels. Counseling may be a good option as well, but if you opt to go this route, then be sure to meet the counselor first and be sure he or she understands the effects of narcissistic abuse.

Your child also needs to know that it is perfectly acceptable to be angry at the narcissist, even if that person is her father or some other adult close to her. In many Christian circles, anger is condemned or said is from the devil. The real truth though is that anger is an emotion, and all emotions are from God. This means it cannot be a bad thing! Only good things come from God, as is stated in James 1:17 *"Every good gift and every perfect gift is from above..."* *(KJV)* The bad thing about anger is when a person does something bad with it. If a person gets angry and kills another, that is bad. But, if a person is angry with another person, makes changes in order to protect herself, then works through their anger and forgives that person, that is certainly good. Anger has its place, just like other emotions.

Talk to your child about forgiveness, too, not just anger. She has the right to be angry about what happened to her. After all, abuse is always wrong. Even so, when she is ready, she needs to forgive the narcissist. Not because that person deserves her forgiveness. Obviously, he does not, but your child deserves to be happy. It is impossible to be happy if she carries anger around inside of her.

Forgiving that person also does not mean she has to continue to be in a relationship with the narcissist if she does not want to be, so be sure to tell your child that. She does not need to have the false belief that so many people have of forgiving always means forgetting, and continuing the relationship the way things were. Forgiveness simply means that she is no longer angry at the person who abused her.

Be a safe haven for your child. Pray for her and with her. Be the person she can run to and know she can talk to about anything. Listen quietly when she wants to talk. Only offer advice when asked. If she does not ask for advice, you know your child - you can tell if she is open to it or not even if she has not said anything. Even if you think she is open, ask before offering advice. "Do you want to know what I think?" "I have an idea... do you want to hear it?" are a couple of ways you can do that.

When your child is talking about the narcissist, always remember to stay as calm as possible. Your calm demeanor will help to keep your child calm. If you get upset, she will become even more upset than she already was. She needs your stability.

Offer your child frequent praise. Praise will help to build her up and hopefully to repair some of the damage to her self-esteem.

When you must offer constructive criticism, do so gently. Do not tell her she is stupid, incapable, a failure or anything judgmental or cruel. Chances are, she has heard enough awful criticisms from the narcissist. Instead, say something like, "I know a way to do that which might work out better (or be easier, etc). Want to try it?" Do not forget to explain why what she did was wrong when appropriate. If what she did still produced good results, but was simply done differently than you would have done it, then you can suggest she try your way next time. If she does not want to, though, respect that decision.

Allow your child to make her own mistakes rather than try to prevent them when possible. Trying to prevent a child from making mistakes makes her insecure. She will grow up believing that she is not smart enough to make her own decisions or maneuver through life.

She is already insecure enough after dealing with narcissistic abuse, and does not need anything else to make her feel more insecure.

As I mentioned earlier, emotional incest is very common when a child is raised by at least one narcissistic parent, but it also can happen with a narcissistic grandparent, aunt, uncle or other older relatives. Although it may not sound so bad, I can tell you from personal experience as well as experiences my readers have told me about, emotional incest is nothing to take lightly! **A person who puts a child in the place of being emotionally responsible for them is abusing that child!**

Emotional incest usually starts when the child is very young. The parent usually confides in her about marital or sexual problems or other things that should be discussed with another adult such as the spouse, a good friend or even a counselor. Saying things like, "I can't talk to anyone else about this" or encouraging secrets between that parent and child that the other parent is not to know about also constitute emotional incest.

Such abusive actions ingrain a deep sense of responsibility in the child regarding the emotional well-being of the parent. This also can create potentially devastating problems for the child. She may feel depressed, anxious, or feel guilty constantly. If her parent is upset, she will work hard to make that parent happy. She may try to be the perfect child, never upsetting her parents, and then suddenly turn rebellious in her teen years. As an adult, she may battle addiction or have poor relationship skills. She may be an overly demanding wife and mother, ignoring her husband's and children's needs and wants. She may continue to keep her emotionally incestuous parent as her top priority, leaving her husband and children to feel abandoned. She may even have a fear of intimacy.

Emotionally incestuous parents also make terrible in-laws, so as an adult, the child may feel caught in the middle between the man she loves and the parent she is close to yet who disapproves so vehemently of her husband. Her husband also may feel like an outsider, because when in his father in-law's presence, he is deliberately excluded. Or, the father only calls his daughter when he knows her husband is not home.

Dealing with the damage of emotional incest is not easy, but it is possible. As the child's parent, naturally it is your duty to protect your child and to help her deal with this incredibly painful situation.

First, your child needs to know that this is wrong. It may be hard to accept at first. She may feel special because the narcissist talks to her like a grown up even though she is only a child. She needs to know that although she may feel special, that does not mean it is good for her. She is still a child, and should enjoy being one without having the responsibility of being the emotional caregiver of an adult in her life.

Once she accepts this, then she will need to deal with her feelings. Let her know she is able to talk to you about anything. Give her a pretty diary where she can write out anything she wants. If you have a close friend or relative that is safe and would be willing to listen, let her know she can talk to that person anytime. Counseling may be an excellent option as well. Offer to pray with her and encourage her to talk to God about her feelings.

Let your child know that it is perfectly OK to tell the narcissist that she does not want to talk about a subject that makes her uncomfortable. Tell her to change the subject. If, like many narcissists, he ignores her and continues his dysfunctional behavior, tell her to keep changing the subject. Eventually most narcissists will get tired of fighting and drop the subject.

Your child may decide she wants to spend less time with the emotionally incestuous narcissist. Let her do as she is comfortable. If you are separated or divorced and sharing custody, this may be very hard to do. Try to respect her wishes as much as you can. Talk to your attorney about how to make sure she spends less time with her narcissistic parent.

You should pray about whether or not to discuss this situation with the emotionally incestuous narcissist, and how to do so if talking about it is your decision. Since narcissists can be so difficult to deal with, you need to use your own discernment on this. Will this person get angry with you and keep that anger between you two, or will he take it out on your child?

And, tell your child that this is not her fault. She has done nothing wrong. The person who has treated her this way made a bad choice by talking to her about inappropriate subject matter, but that does not mean she has done something wrong or is a bad child. **Being abused is never the victim's fault!**

Lastly, always be sure to pray for your child. Ask God to heal her, to make her whole.

Chapter Three - Helping Your Child Avoid Further Narcissistic Abuse

As anyone who has experience with narcissists knows, there is no way to prevent narcissistic abuse completely. There are a great many narcissists in the world today, so it is a guarantee that you will run into at least a couple in your life. Plus, as mentioned earlier, those who have been through abuse are often sought after by abusers. Abusers of all types are very good at selecting their victims. Someone who has been abused before often can be abused again. (Think about a woman who leaves her abusive husband only later to marry another man who abuses her.) Even so, there are some things that your child can do to minimize the possibility of facing further narcissistic abuse in the future.

Most importantly, pray. When your child is forced to deal with a narcissist, encourage her to pray about the best way to handle the situation. She will be pleasantly surprised by the creative ideas God places in her heart.

Encourage very open, honest communication with your child. If she is unsure about his new friend at school, she needs to know that she can come to you with any questions, concerns or problems. If something her grandmother wants her to do makes her feel bad somehow, she should be able to come to you to discuss it. Your child needs to know that she can talk to you about anything without fear of judgment or criticism, and if you must correct her, you will do so lovingly.

Spotting narcissists is essential. Once you have taught your child about Narcissistic Personality Disorder, she should be able to do this fairly easily. Once she can do that, she can know who to avoid when possible and how to deal with the narcissists she cannot avoid.

Also very important is teaching your child about how to set and enforce healthy boundaries. This will be discussed in more detail in the following chapter.

Be a good example for your child about how to deal with narcissists. Show your child that you do not quietly tolerate being abused by setting and enforcing healthy boundaries, no matter who the narcissist is, even if that narcissist is your spouse or parent. Do your best to keep your emotions under control when dealing with the narcissist, especially in front of your child. Narcissists feed off anger and hurt in their victims, so obviously being upset will encourage him to continue to hurt you while also upsetting your child. If you decide to end the relationship with the narcissist, explain why to your child. This can be tricky, because if that narcissist is your spouse, the child does not need to know all of the intimate details of your marriage. Asking God for discernment and wisdom on what to share will help you a great deal.

Also, if your child has to continue to deal with the narcissist, remind her that people with Narcissistic Personality Disorder are not like most people. The things you expect from most people, you cannot expect from a narcissist. For example, if you are sad, you can expect most people to care, to ask what is wrong and to offer you comfort. Narcissists are not like that. They do not have the ability to care that you are hurting. They are too focused on caring about themselves to be bothered with the fact that someone else is hurting or hurting another person makes them feel good. If you expect them to care that you are upset, you will be disappointed every time when they show they do not care. The same goes if you think that they will stop bragging about themselves or stop using people for their own benefit. The simple fact is narcissists very rarely change, and when they do, usually it is only temporary and only to benefit the narcissist in some way. Accepting the narcissist as he is helps, because your child will not be constantly disappointed when she hopes this time will be better. (Accepting him as he is does not mean she needs to accept being abused, however!)

I recently stumbled across a very helpful tool in dealing with narcissists that may help you and your child as well. Interestingly, I read about it regarding showing care givers how to deal compassionately with people with advanced Alzheimer's disease, but I have found that it also works with narcissists. When a narcissist is upsetting you, take a deep breath. That helps to calm you down a bit, and gives you a moment to think of a reasonable response instead of simply reacting out of anger or hurt. It is always best to respond instead of react when dealing with narcissists because the more upset you are, the more they realize they can control you and the more they will attempt to control you. It also makes them feel good about themselves when they see that they have the ability, the power, to make someone act so irrationally. Do not give them that power! Take that deep breath, relax, and respond, and teach your child to do the same.

Chapter Four - Teaching Children About Boundaries

Boundaries are an essential part of life, but perhaps they are no more important than when it comes to dealing with narcissistic people. If your boundaries are weak or non-existent, a narcissist will be more than happy to walk all over you any time the mood strikes.

As a parent, a part of that job includes teaching your child about how to have and enforce healthy boundaries. This comes naturally to many people, but certainly not to everyone. Those of us raised by narcissistic or abusive parents naturally have very weak boundaries, if we have any at all, so we often know nothing or very little on the topic until we finally realize that we need to make some changes.

Teaching your child about boundaries may benefit you as well. After all, if you are going to teach something, you need to have knowledge on the topic yourself. Even if you already know about boundaries, you still may learn something if you study them in order to teach your child.

To start teaching about boundaries, you need to understand the basics about boundaries. Boundaries define what you are and are not responsible for. They are like a fence surrounding your yard. The things within your fence are what you are responsible for, such as your feelings, actions and beliefs. The feelings, actions and beliefs of other people are inside their fences, and outside of yours. This means you are not responsible for those things. In fact, you do not even need to have an opinion of such things. If someone is doing something hurtful or dangerous, of course you can try to speak to them gently and lovingly about such things. Ephesians 4:15 encourages us to "speak the truth in love." However, if what they do, feel or believe simply disagrees with your preference, then it is simply none of your business. Everyone is entitled to live their life on their terms so long as they do not hurt others in the process.

It can be very helpful to have a friend (or a couple of friends) who already know about boundaries to help you during this time. They can encourage you when you are doing well, and correct you when you make a mistake.

If you are starting to set boundaries for the first time, some people may call you selfish, mean or other not so nice things. They may try to push or even ignore your boundaries. These are signs of unsafe people. Safe people only want the best for you, and they know that boundaries are a good thing. Safe people will be very proud of you for learning about boundaries, especially if you have never done so before.

You are going to need to start to say no sometimes. It may feel very foreign at first, but you will get the hang of it! You do not need to do as you are told to do every single time. You do not need to assist someone every single time that you are asked. You absolutely have the right to say no if you are unable, unwilling or even just uncomfortable.

Remember, "no" can be a complete sentence. You do not owe people a detailed explanation, especially if you are not comfortable giving one.

You will need to figure out good ways to enforce your newly formed boundaries. This may be very difficult to do at first, but it gets easier with practice. If someone continues to discuss something after

17

you have said you do not wish to talk about it any longer, the simplest way to handle the uncomfortable situation is to change the subject. If the person changes it back, then you change it again. Most people will give up after a couple of subject changes. Also, you can use boundary setting phrases, such as:

- "I won't do that."
- "You are entitled to your opinion, but I am entitled to have my opinion as well."
- "I'm not going to discuss this topic anymore." Then change the subject, refusing to go back to the original topic.

Some boundary-resistant people are especially hard to deal with. For them, you may need to hang up the phone, leave the room or walk away from them if they refuse to respect your boundary.

I strongly recommend reading the book, "Boundaries" by Drs. Henry Cloud and John Townsend. The book changed my life! In fact, it inspired me to write a free course based on the book. It is available on my website at this link: http://cynthiabaileyrug.com/Boundaries-Book-Study.php

Once you become familiar with boundaries, it is time to teach your child what you have learned. If your child is of an appropriate age, you may want her to read the above mentioned book, if she is willing. You could discuss it together. However, if this is not a possibility, then you can share with her what you have learned in the book.

Be a good role model of having and enforcing healthy boundaries. Children learn a great deal from watching their parents. If you are a good example of someone with healthy boundaries, they will learn much more from watching you than they could learn from anything you tell them.

Make sure your child knows what is and is not her responsibility. Remember, beliefs, feelings and actions are the responsibility of each individual.

Teach your child that it is perfectly fine to say no sometimes, and teach her various ways to say no respectfully yet firmly.

Do not push your child's boundaries. Respect them instead. For example, if you tell your young child to hug Grandma but she does not want to, she has that right. Respecting a child's boundaries teaches her that her boundaries deserve to be respected. Ignoring them teaches her that she does not have the right to boundaries, which can make her an easy target for abusers. Abusive people look for children with weak boundaries since they make the easiest victims.

Help your child to honor her own boundaries. If she is shy, for example, do not criticize that quality or try to push her into being more social. Respect that boundary, even if you are the opposite way. Your child does not need to feel as if something is wrong with her or her boundaries are wrong when nothing could be further from the truth!

When you set boundaries with your child, do so in an appropriate manner. Do so calmly and reasonably. A parent who consistently sets boundaries in a harsh manner may create a child who sets his boundaries harshly instead of in a healthy way.

Be consistent, firm and reasonable with your boundaries with your child. Do not be lax with them or fail to follow through on enforcing them. That type of behavior teaches your children that boundaries are meant to be broken and you are not serious about your boundaries.

As always, let your child know she can come to you with any questions. Have open, honest dialog. If you are new to boundaries too, then be willing to learn together. Tell your child, "I don't know, but I will find out" if you do not know how to answer her question, and, make sure you find out the answer she is seeking. I firmly believe people of all ages respect a person who is real. If you admit that you do not know the answer your child wants but are willing to figure it out, she will respect that a great deal more than if you fake knowing the answer. People, especially children, can smell someone who is not being genuine a mile away, and most people do not like fake. They certainly do not respect fake. Pretending you know an answer you do not can cause your child to lose some respect for you.

Chapter Five - When The Narcissist Is Someone Close

Narcissistic friends and relatives can be extremely difficult to deal with, especially when you have children to protect. In this chapter, we will discuss some ways to deal with these people while keeping your child safe.

Narcissistic grandparents are a very common phenomenon these days, so for the sake of simplicity, we will refer to narcissists as grandparents in this chapter. The information provided is still appropriate for family, friends, aunts, uncles or any other narcissist however.

Chances are you have heard about some narcissistic grandparents. I have heard stories of grandparents who dislike the woman their son married or man their daughter married, so they made false accusations of abuse to get the grandchildren taken away from their parents. Some have even had the hated in-law killed or killed the person themselves. In less severe (but still very damaging to their grandchildren) cases, they bad mouth the parent they dislike to their grandchild and start strife between that child and her parents. My mother's mother did that. She told my mother that my father and I were "plotting against her" many times. Naturally this was very upsetting to my mother, who, after hearing it, would confront my father and I who were simply baffled by the accusation. My grandmother also told me what a terrible daughter my mother was when she was growing up. According to her, my mother was lazy and useless. She did this when I was very young, too young to know this was not something to tell my mother. Unfortunately, when my mother would ask me what my grandmother and I talked about, I told her, which hurt her deeply.

People do not start out being narcissistic grandparents, however. They were narcissistic parents first. What they did to you, chances are they may do to your child as well, often for the sole purpose of hurting you, and you will have to work hard to protect your child.

In typical narcissist style, narcissists want control over their grandchild, and will do anything they think will accomplish that control. They often use guilt to induce dysfunctional, codependent behavior ("I need you!" "That's ok.. you just do what you want. I'll get by somehow…" "I guess you have better things to do than spend time with me."). They also use threats frequently. Threats are not always verbal, as I mentioned previously. In fact, threats are usually not verbal with narcissists, especially when the narcissist is older, such as in the case of narcissistic grandparents. A dirty look, body language or a specific tone of voice can be very threatening when a person knows something bad easily can accompany the look, body language or tone of voice. Most narcissists also withdraw their love and affection to gain control. The silent treatment is an old favorite of most narcissistic parents and grandparents. It causes a great deal of pain and confusion. The silent treatment encourages the person on the receiving end of the silent treatment to ask what is wrong and to work hard to make the narcissist talk to them again. It is a very effective weapon, at least until the victim realizes what is happening and begins to enjoy the break from the narcissistic drama (that is where I am with it. I enjoy the silent treatment when my narcissistic mother uses it. It is a nice break for me! As a child however, it was extremely distressing! It took me well into my thirties before I realized how good the silent treatment could be for me.)

Narcissistic grandparents are not immune to creating an emotionally incestuous or parentalizing situation, and it can be just as damaging as it is when a parent does it. Rather than repeat the information in this chapter, please review it in chapter two entitled, "Repairing The Damage."

Narcissistic grandparents also like to bribe their grandchild. Chances are, they are financially stable by this time in their life, and can afford to give their grandchild expensive toys or even cash in an attempt to gain control over the grandchild.

If they are not financially stable, they may try to get money from their grandchild or adult child by pretending they are going without important things such as food or medication. In fact, some have been known to do this even when they have a great deal of money in the bank.

Many narcissistic grandparents like to contact their grandchild behind the parents' back, such as via email or texting. It may be a good idea to block your parents' email or phone number on your child's cell phone. If your child is too young for either, monitor anything that comes in the mail to your child from your parents. You are the parent, and you have that right!

Be sure to let your child know, as always, that she can come to you with any concerns or questions. Let her know that you are on her side, and will protect her from her grandparents.

In many cases, someone can tolerate abuse from their parents until they have a child. When they see the child going through the same things they did from their parents, it becomes too much and they decide to go no contact with their parents. If you end up deciding to do this, you will need to explain it to your child who may be wondering why Grandma and Grandpa are no longer allowed to talk to them. First, remember that you are the parent. You get to make this decision. You do not need to apologize for your decision or over-justify it. Second, reassure your child that you have made the best decision for your child as well as yourself. Yes, it hurts, but this was the wisest and most loving thing to do under the circumstances. You cannot let this person hurt you or your child any longer.

If you have opted to go no contact, your child may one day decide to have a relationship with this person. You need to prepare for this possibility, since it can be very hurtful. It is your child's right to contact the person once she is of age though. And, chances are slim that it is done for the sole purpose of hurting you. It may be done simply out of curiosity. Your child may wonder exactly what this grandparent did that made you decide to go no contact. She probably wonders what this person is really like, and want to find out for herself.

I did this. My mother stopped speaking to her mother when I was fourteen years old. Not long after I turned eighteen, I started speaking to my grandmother. My mother, being a narcissist like her mother, did not take it well. She did not understand me speaking to her mother when she was not, and was livid when someone told her I had visited my grandmother. My mother screamed at me and called me a traitor for going behind her back to speak to my grandmother, even though I hid it trying to protect my mother. Yet soon after this incident, she began having a relationship with her mother again. It was never a good one, though, even when she was one of her mother's care givers the last few years of her life.

To this day, over twenty-six years later, I feel bad for hurting my mother so badly and basically setting the stage for her to reenter such a dysfunctional, abusive situation with her mother. My grandmother was a cruel, evil, heartless woman who abused my mother until the day she died. Unfortunately, when I first began talking to her, I had hoped she would be nice to me, like my other grandmother was. (Yes, I was very naïve!) I also did not think my mother would find out I was speaking to her mother. I was wrong on both counts.

24

If your child opts to rekindle a relationship with the narcissist you tried to protect her from, remember, you have every right to maintain no contact if that is your desire. Your child befriending the person does not mean you have to befriend him as well.

You also are within your rights to tell your child in a respectful you do not wish to hear about that person. You wish your child well in this relationship, but do not care to hear about him.

Narcissists love triangulation, where they use another person to get to you. If that happens and your child is being used by the narcissist to triangulate, refuse to engage in it. Remind your child that you do not wish to discuss this person.

Chapter Six - Raising Children With A Narcissist

Lastly are some tips for the person who is in the unenviable position of trying to raise happy, healthy children with a narcissist.

You are in one of the most challenging positions a parent can face. Chances are, it feels like an impossible situation, but with God's help and exercising some skills on your part, you and your child can get through this.

If you still live with the narcissistic parent, the best advice I can give you is to get out as soon as humanly possible. Protect yourself and your child(ren)! If the narcissist is also physically or sexually abusive, you stand a very good chance of getting a restraining order. Granted, they are merely a piece of paper to many abusers, but having one will, at the very least, prove to the legal system that this person is dangerous. That can work in your favor.

Document EVERYTHING and keep it well hidden from the narcissist. Documentation will come in handy for several reasons. First, it will help you to keep everything straight. Living with a narcissist, that can be difficult to do sometimes since they love to gaslight their victims, keeping them confused at all times. Second, seeing things in writing helps to make it real. Many narcissists go too far, then begin treating their victims well for a time to lure them back in. This can create a feeling of doubt:

> "He is being so good to us now, how could I have been so angry with him?"

> "I probably was just overreacting. He did not mean to say or do what he did."

> "He really is a good guy. He is probably right, and I just tend to be too sensitive sometimes."

Seeing the things he has done to you and your child in writing will dispel that doubt. There is something about seeing your story in black and white that makes it more real. Memories can be manipulated, but words on paper (or on a document on your computer) cannot. What you wrote is what will be on that paper or computer unless you change it.

Documenting everything also will help you if you get a divorce. If the police are involved, and usually they are when dealing with a narcissist, you can show them that your spouse has a history of being abusive. A one time event may not get their attention, but a history of abuse will. Documentation may help you to get a restraining order as well.

If you lose custody of your child to the narcissistic parent, you are going to need to stay as calm and collected around your child and your ex as possible. Chances are, your ex is telling your child what a terrible, unstable person you are, so if you act out, this will prove to your child that the narcissist is right. That person then can say to your child, "See? I told you she was crazy!" I am sure you easily can envision your ex creating a scenario for you to be upset while he stays calm, then saying something like that to your child.

Do not discuss your marriage to your child. Your child is still a child, after all, and does not need to know all of the details of an adult situation like this. Especially when it involves her parents. You can answer questions as you feel are appropriate however, and when you do, always do so in a matter of fact way, without accusations and blame. No child will respond well to badmouthing their parent, whether or not what is said is true. Most children are protective of their parents. Narcissists like to exploit that in their child, making their child even more protective. If you say anything negative to your child about the other parent, no matter how true, chances are good it will backfire on you, and she will become angry with you.

Do not try to prove your innocence to your child. Let your actions speak for themselves. Your child will pay close attention to your actions. Children watch everything and miss nothing. Live your life as normally as possible. Listen when she speaks. Laugh with her when she is happy and comfort her when she is sad. Pray with and for your child. Do fun things together. Behave as the good person and good parent that you are, and your child will not believe lies the narcissistic parent may say. Even if your child believes the lies for a time, the truth always comes out at some point. Trust God to help your child to see the truth if this happens. Pray for her to see the truth.

If your child has fallen for the lies of her narcissistic parent, as hard as it is, try not to resent your child. Narcissists are great actors, and can fool anyone. Remember, you were once fooled, too.

Whether you still live with your narcissistic spouse or not, do not spoil your child! It can be natural to want to do so, but in the end, it causes problems. A child that has one narcissistic parent and one over-indulging one can turn out to be narcissistic. Instead, just continue to be a good parent.

Teach your child that while it seems like her narcissistic parent gets whatever he wants by his bad behavior that does not make it a good thing. It is much better to be a Godly person, to be good, polite and empathetic. Treating people right means people will often treat you well, too. People will want to be around you, they will love you, and they will respect you. While many narcissists brag about how well-respected they are, the truth is people do not respect them - they fear them. Respect is so much better than fear!

Do not try to get your child to behave a certain way to appease the narcissistic parent. This always backfires, because narcissists always change the rules. What worked yesterday will not work today, but it may work again next week. No one can please a narcissist, no matter how hard they try. Also, trying to please the narcissistic parent can set your child up to become a narcissist. She sees how hard others work to please the narcissist, and unconsciously decides that since it works so well for him, she will do it too. It is not a guarantee she will become a narcissist, but it certainly increases her chances greatly.

Children need more than clothing, food and shelter. They also need unconditional love, respect, reasonable discipline, freedom to be who they are and yes, even fun. They need parents who are balanced and consistent. When they are forced to deal with adult situations such as narcissistic abuse, they cannot process it well. Their brains are simply not as developed as that of adults, therefore they are not as equipped to deal with adult matters. They need help from a parent who provides them with the things mentioned above.

Teach your child to be a good person. You can do this mostly be your behavior. By you being devoted in your faith, compassionate, willing to help those in need and generous, you will show your child by actions how to be a good person. This will help your child to be a good person, since children learn so much by watching their parents.

Chapter Seven – Just For Parents

You cannot focus on your child every single moment. You also need to take care of yourself, if for no other reason than to enable you to take care of your child. Do not neglect yourself! Be sure to take care of your physical health and your emotional health. It may be a good idea to seek counseling with a counselor familiar with Narcissistic Personality Disorder and narcissistic abuse. There are some counselors familiar with narcissism, but not as many as I wish there were. You may need to see a few before finding a counselor you feel can understand your situation. If you need help finding one, you can do a search online for local counselors with this area of expertise. Or, if you are unable to afford counseling, check with your local churches. Many offer Christian counseling free or very low cost. Your local Department of Mental Health also offers free and low cost counseling.

If counseling is not something you may be interested in, try keeping a journal. (I mean something separate from the documentation you are keeping. A safe place where you not only document events, but get your feelings out as well.) If you are afraid of someone finding it, then try keeping one online. There are many free, private, password protected online journal sites available. I use one myself. Journaling can be very helpful. It provides a safe place to get your feelings out. Plus, an added bonus is as I mentioned earlier in this chapter, and writing helps to validate your pain by making what happened more real. You will know beyond a shadow of a doubt that yes, things really were that bad and you also will know exactly what you are trying to heal from. You cannot heal from something if you do not know what is wrong. I wrote my autobiography, "Emerging from the Chrysalis" in 2012. It was extremely painful but also extremely helpful. For the first time, I realized exactly how bad my experiences have been and exactly how strong I am for surviving them. It was eye opening. Your journal can do the same thing for you.

Do you have safe, caring friends or relatives you can talk to? Then do not forget to recruit their help sometimes. Not only will they listen if you need to talk, but they may offer help. Maybe they will baby sit so you can enjoy a night off or take you to lunch to help get your mind off of things. Safe and caring people are an absolute blessing!

Never forget, pray pray and pray some more! As much of a blessing as good people can be, God is infinitely better. He helps to heal you and comfort you. He gives you wisdom and insight when you need it. He provides all of your needs. Rely on Him, and you will get through this painful situation with your head held high.

Epilogue

It is never easy dealing with a narcissist, and it can be even harder when you also have a child to protect. I pray God grants everyone who reads this book the strength, wisdom, courage and anything else you need to be able to help your child however he or she needs! I also pray this book has given you some tools that will help you find new and useful ways to help and protect your child.

Again, I would like to stress an important point. While taking care of your child, please do not forget to take care of yourself too. Dealing with narcissists and the effects of narcissistic abuse can be incredibly draining of your energy and potentially your physical and mental health as well. Take good care of yourself. Rest as you need to. Ask for help if you need it. Talk about how you feel with a safe person and write in your journal. Do what you need to do to take good care of your physical and mental health. You are not being selfish for doing that, you are being smart! Your child needs you, and you cannot be there for her if you are falling apart emotionally or are sickly. Taking care of yourself is a gift not only for yourself, but your child as well.

Do not forget to distract yourself and your child, too. No one can think about such a depressing topic as narcissism constantly without becoming depressed. Make sure that you and your child take time where you deliberately do not focus on what has happened. Have fun! Play games, go to the park or go somewhere else you both enjoy. Be silly together. Laugh a lot. Enjoy your life! Jesus came to the Earth for many reasons, one of which is so that you may enjoy your life, so why not enjoy it to the fullest?

John 10:10 "The thief cometh not, but for to steal, and to kill, and to destroy: I am come that they might have life, and that they might have it more abundantly." (KJV)

With Love,
Cynthia

About The Author

Cynthia Bailey-Rug is happily married to Eric Rug. Together they live outside Annapolis, Maryland with their menagerie of lovely pets.

Cynthia has been a Christian since 1996, and believes God has called her to write. She always loved writing, but realized it was her purpose in 2003. She has since written many articles and books. She also has edited books for other up and coming authors. She enjoys reading, animals, classic cars, crafts, gardening, electronic gadgets, and spending time with her friends, family and pets.

Where To Find Cynthia Bailey-Rug Online

Website: www.CynthiaBaileyRug.com

Facebook fan group:
https://www.facebook.com/groups/FansOfCynthiaBaileyRug/

Twitter: https://twitter.com/CynthiaRug

Blog: https://cynthiabaileyrug.wordpress.com/

Linkedin: https://www.linkedin.com/in/cynthiabaileyrug

Tumblr: http://www.tumblr.com/blog/cynthiabaileyrug

Google+: https://plus.google.com/+CynthiaBaileyRug

Amazon: http://amazon.com/author/cynthiabaileyrug

Smashwords:
https://www.smashwords.com/profile/view/CynthiaBaileyRug

Made in the USA
Coppell, TX
30 December 2020

47305453R10032